CW00880724

WOMEN'S SUFFRAGE

BY SETH LYNCH

Gareth Stevens
PUBLISHING

CRASHCOURSE

Please visit our website, www.garethstevens.com. For a free color catalog of all our high-quality books, call toll free 1-800-542-2595 or fax 1-877-542-2596.

Library of Congress Cataloging-in-Publication Data

Names: Lynch, Seth, author.
Title: Women's suffrage / Seth Lynch.
Description: New York : Gareth Stevens Publishing, 2019. | Series: A look at US history | Includes index.
Identifiers: LCCN 2017054293| ISBN 9781538221358 (library bound) | ISB 9781538221372 (pbk.) | ISBN 9781538221389 (6 pack)
Subjects: LCSH: Women--Suffrage--United States--History--Juvenile literature.
| Suffragists--United States--History--Juvenile literature. | United States. Constitution. 19th Amendment--History--Juvenile literature.
Classification: LCC JK1898 .L96 2019 | DDC 324.6/230973--dc23 LC record available at https://lccn.loc.gov/2017054293

First Edition

Published in 2019 by
Gareth Stevens Publishing
111 East 14th Street, Suite 349
New York, NY 10003

Designer: Samantha DeMartin
Editor: Kristen Nelson

Photo credits: Series art Christophe BOISSON/Shutterstock.com; (feather quill) Galushko Sergey/Shutterstock.com; (parchment) mollicart-design/Shutterstock.com; cover, p. 1 F. J. Mortimer/Hulton Archive/Getty Images; p. 5 Topical Press Agency/Hulton Archive/Getty Images; pp. 7, 13 Everett Historical/Shutterstock.com; pp. 9, 15 Bettmann/ Bettmann/Getty Images; pp. 11, 27 Universal History Archive/Universal Images Group/ Getty Images; pp. 17, 21, 23, 25 courtesy of the Library of Congress; p. 19 Library of Congress/ Corbis Historical/Getty Images; p. 29 Joe Raedle/Getty Images News/Getty Images.

Printed in the United States of America

CPSIA compliance information: Batch #CS18GS: For further information contact Gareth Stevens, New York, New York at 1-800-542-2595.

CONTENTS

Words in the glossary appear in **bold** type the first time they are used in the text.

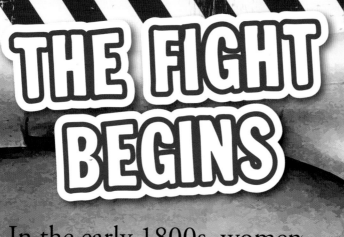

THE FIGHT BEGINS

In the early 1800s, women wanted to make changes in the United States. However, those in government wouldn't listen to them because women didn't have suffrage, or the right to vote. Women across the country came together to **demand** this right.

MAKE THE GRADE

The first leaders of the women's suffrage movement,
Elizabeth Cady Stanton and Lucretia Mott, met while
working in the **abolitionist** movement.

CHAIRMAN
Mrs M.ROBERTSON
SPEAKER
Mrs FAWCETT

10

NATIONAL UNION of WOMEN'S SUFFRAGE SOCIETIES
PRESIDENT Mrs FAWCETT
LAW-ABIDING SUFFRAGISTS

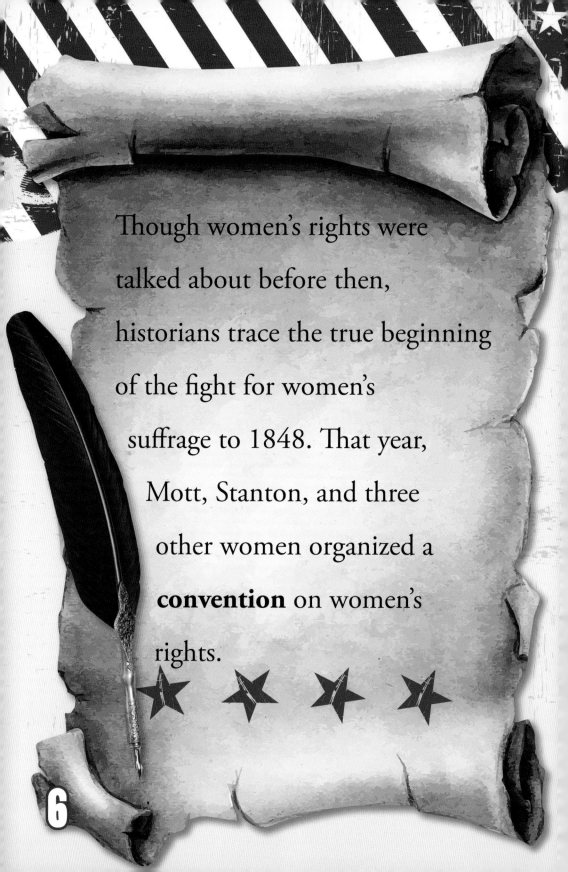

Though women's rights were talked about before then, historians trace the true beginning of the fight for women's suffrage to 1848. That year, Mott, Stanton, and three other women organized a **convention** on women's rights.

Elizabeth Cady Stanton

MAKE THE GRADE

Elizabeth Cady Stanton was born in 1815. She had more schooling than most girls of the time and also learned about law from her father.

7

THE SENECA FALLS CONVENTION

The women placed ads in the newspaper to let others know about the meeting. News of the convention also traveled by word of mouth. More than 300 people came! The convention occurred on July 19 and 20, 1848, in Seneca Falls, New York.

MAKE THE GRADE

Both men and women went to the
Seneca Falls Convention.

Elizabeth Cady Stanton and Women's Rights

Stanton presented a **document** called the Declaration of Sentiments that stated the rights women should have. It asked for the right to schooling and treatment under the law equal to men. It also demanded the right to vote in government.

THE FIRST CONVENTION

EVER CALLED TO DISCUSS THE

Civil and Political Rights of Women,

SENECA FALLS, N. Y., JULY 19, 20, 1848.

WOMAN'S RIGHTS CONVENTION.

A Convention to discuss the social, civil, and religious condition and rights of woman will be held in the Wesleyan Chapel, at Seneca Falls, N. Y., on Wednesday and Thursday, the 19th and 20th of July current; commencing at 10 o'clock A. M. During the first day the meeting will be exclusively for women, who are earnestly invited to attend. The public generally are invited to be present on the second day, when Lucretia Mott, of Philadelphia, and other ladies and gentlemen, will address the Convention.*

MAKE THE GRADE

One hundred people—68 women and 32 men—signed the Declaration of Sentiments, including well-known abolitionist Frederick Douglass!

THE MOVEMENT SPREADS

Other conventions followed the one at Seneca Falls. The first national women's rights convention was held in Massachusetts in 1850. In 1852, Stanton planned another convention with Susan B. Anthony. These meetings made it clear that the call for women's suffrage was growing in strength.

Susan B. Anthony

MAKE THE GRADE

Anthony was born in 1820. She also took part in the abolitionist movement before meeting Stanton and joining the fight for women's right to vote.

STOP FOR WAR

When the **Civil War** began in 1861, the fight for women's suffrage stopped for a time. Many women, including Stanton and Anthony, worked in favor of the Thirteenth **Amendment**, which would end slavery. It passed, and the war ended in 1865.

MAKE THE GRADE

Stanton and Anthony found 400,000 people to sign a paper in favor of passing the Thirteenth Amendment!

AMENDMENT SETBACKS

After the Civil War, two amendments opened up voting rights. The Fourteenth Amendment gave all adult men the right to vote. The Fifteenth Amendment made it illegal to stop men from voting because of their race. But, their wording **excluded** women from voting.

MAKE THE GRADE

The Fourteenth Amendment was the first part of the
US **Constitution** to use the word "male."

Following these amendments, Stanton and Anthony started the National Woman Suffrage Association. They worked for a national law giving women suffrage. The American Woman Suffrage Association, formed by Lucy Stone and Julia Ward Howe, worked toward state laws giving women suffrage.

MAKE THE GRADE

In 1890, the two groups joined to become the National American Woman Suffrage Association (NAWSA).

ANTHONY VOTES

In November 1872, Anthony and 15 other women voted in New York State. They were all **arrested**, but only Anthony faced a trial. The judge said the wording of the Fourteenth Amendment made it illegal for women to vote.

MAKE THE GRADE

The judge told Anthony she had to pay $100 for her actions. Anthony said she would "never pay a dollar" of it!

AN AMENDMENT IN CONGRESS

A women's suffrage amendment was first presented in Congress in 1878. It didn't pass. But, the National Woman Suffrage Association tried to reintroduce it several times after that. By the late 1800s, it had started to gain favor in Congress.

MAKE THE GRADE

In the late 1800s and early 1900s, many states began giving women the right to vote. Members of Congress, therefore, were partly **elected** by women. So, they began to vote in favor of women's suffrage.

LEADERS ARISE

The women's suffrage movement needed new, younger leaders as the 1900s began. Carrie Chapman Catt became president of the NAWSA in 1915. Alice Paul, another suffragist, left the NAWSA because she wanted to take more action in the fight for women's voting rights.

Alice Paul

MAKE THE GRADE

Paul formed the National Women's Party. They held marches and even **hunger strikes** in their fight for the right to vote.

25

THE RIGHT TO VOTE!

The Nineteenth Amendment, which gave women the right to vote, passed in the House of **Representatives** in January 1918. It then passed in the Senate in June 1919. The amendment needed to be **ratified** by three-fourths of the states.

MAKE THE GRADE

The Nineteenth Amendment was ratified by enough states in August 1920. It became part of the US Constitution!

27

The Nineteenth Amendment says it's illegal to stop someone from voting based on their sex. It gave women a voice in government and made that voice equal to men's. After more than 70 years, the fight for women's suffrage was over!

The women's rights movement continued after the passage of the Nineteenth Amendment. Equal pay is just one concern women in the United States still have.

29

TIMELINE OF WOMEN'S SUFFRAGE

1848
The Seneca Falls Convention is held.

1850
The first national women's rights convention occurs.

1861–1865
The US Civil War is fought.

1868
The Fourteenth Amendment gives all men the right to vote.

1870
The Fifteenth Amendment makes it illegal to stop someone from voting because of race.

1872
Susan B. Anthony votes in New York State.

1878
A women's suffrage amendment is first presented in Congress.

1918–1919
The Nineteenth Amendment passes in both houses of Congress.

1920
The Nineteenth Amendment is ratified.

GLOSSARY

abolitionist: one who fights to end slavery

amendment: a change or addition to a constitution

arrest: to be taken in by the police

Civil War: a war fought from 1861 to 1865 in the United States between the Union (the Northern states) and the Confederacy (the Southern states)

constitution: the basic laws by which a country or state is governed

convention: a gathering of people who have a common interest or purpose

demand: to ask forcefully

document: a formal piece of writing

elect: to choose for a position in a government

exclude: to leave out

hunger strike: the act of refusing to eat as a way of showing you disagree with something

ratify: to give formal approval to something

representative: a member of a lawmaking body who acts for voters

FOR MORE INFORMATION

Books

Kent, Deborah. *Elizabeth Cady Stanton: Founder of the Women's Suffrage Movement*. New York, NY: Enslow Publishing, 2017.

Litwin, Laura Baskes. *Susan B. Anthony: Social Reformer and Feminist*. New York, NY: Enslow Publishing, 2017.

Website

Women's Rights National Historical Park: History and Culture

www.nps.gov/wori/learn/historyculture/index.htm

Learn more about the Seneca Falls Convention on the national park's website.

Publisher's note to educators and parents: Our editors have carefully reviewed this website to ensure that it is suitable for students. Many websites change frequently, however, and we cannot guarantee that a site's future contents will continue to meet our high standards of quality and educational value. Be advised that students should be closely supervised whenever they access the internet.

INDEX